# TOOLS FOR CAREGIVERS

- **ATOS:** 0.8
- **GRL:** C
- **WORD COUNT:** 25

- **CURRICULUM CONNECTIONS:** animals, habitats

## Skills to Teach

- **HIGH-FREQUENCY WORDS:** a, at, is, it, look, mom, the, with
- **CONTENT WORDS:** baby, eats, good, gorilla, infant, night, plays, sleeps, stays, walks
- **PUNCTUATION:** exclamation points, periods
- **WORD STUDY:** long /a/, spelled ay (*plays*, *stays*); long /e/, spelled ea (*eats*); long /e/, spelled ee (*sleeps*); short /o/, spelled oo (*good*, *look*); multisyllable words (*baby*, *gorilla*)
- **TEXT TYPE:** information report

## Before Reading Activities

- Read the title and give a simple statement of the main idea.
- Have students "walk" though the book and talk about what they see in the pictures.
- Introduce new vocabulary by having students predict the first letter and locate the word in the text.
- Discuss any unfamiliar concepts that are in the text.

## After Reading Activities

The book tells us that baby gorillas are called infants. Did the readers know this before reading the book? Can they name any other baby animals that have different names than their parents? What are human babies called? Sound out each new word. Write their answers on the board.

Tadpole Books are published by Jump!, 5357 Penn Avenue South, Minneapolis, MN 55419, www.jumplibrary.com

Copyright ©2019 Jump. International copyright reserved in all countries. No part of this book may be reproduced in any form without written permission from the publisher.

**Editor:** Jenna Trnka  **Designer:** Anna Peterson

**Photo Credits:** Asaf Weizman/Shutterstock, cover, 4–5; Gudkov Andrey/Shutterstock, 1; Raffaele Passariello/Dreamstime, 2–3, 16tm; Fitzthum Photography/Shutterstock, 6–7, 16tr; pictures by albi/Shutterstock, 8–9, 16tl; Kiki Dohmeier/Shutterstock, 10–11, 16br; drinhaus/Adobe Stock, 12–13, 16bl; Vladimir Muller/Shutterstock, 14–15, 16bm.

Library of Congress Cataloging-in-Publication Data
Names: Nilsen, Genevieve, author.
Title: Gorilla infants / by Genevieve Nilsen.
Description: Tadpole edition. | Minneapolis, MN : Jump!, Inc., (2019) | Series: Safari babies | Includes index.
Identifiers: LCCN 2018024754 (print) | LCCN 2018027523 (ebook) | ISBN 9781641282420 (ebook) | ISBN 9781641282406 (hardcover : alk. paper) | ISBN 9781641282413 (paperback)
Subjects: LCSH: Gorilla—Infancy—Juvenile literature.
Classification: LCC QL737.P94 (ebook) | LCC QL737.P94 N55 2019 (print) | DDC 599.88413/92—dc23
LC record available at https://lccn.loc.gov/2018024754

## SAFARI BABIES

# GORILLA INFANTS

by Genevieve Nilsen

## TABLE OF CONTENTS

tadpole
books

# GORILLA INFANTS

infant

**Look at the infant!**

It is a baby gorilla.

mom

It stays with mom.

It eats.

It walks.

It plays.

It sleeps. Good night!

# WORDS TO KNOW

eats     infant     mom

plays     sleeps     walks

# INDEX